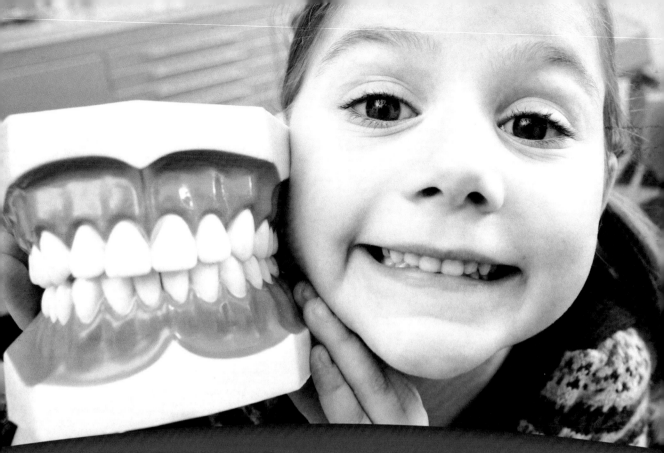

All About Your

TEETH

Jenny Fretland VanVoorst
and Maria Koran

www.av2books.com

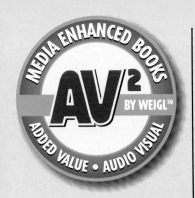

AV² provides enriched content that supplements and complements this book. Weigl's AV² books strive to create inspired learning and engage young minds in a total learning experience.

Your AV² Media Enhanced books come alive with...

Audio
Listen to sections of the book read aloud.

Key Words
Study vocabulary, and complete a matching word activity.

Video
Watch informative video clips.

Quizzes
Test your knowledge.

Embedded Weblinks
Gain additional information for research.

Slide Show
View images and captions, and prepare a presentation.

Try This!
Complete activities and hands-on experiments.

... and much, much more!

Go to **www.av2books.com**, and enter this book's unique code.

BOOK CODE

F 8 3 3 6 3 5

AV² by Weigl brings you media enhanced books that support active learning.

Published by AV² by Weigl
350 5th Avenue, 59th Floor
New York, NY 10118
Website: www.av2books.com

Library of Congress Cataloging-in-Publication Data

Names: Fretland VanVoorst, Jenny, 1972- author. | Koran, Maria, author.
Title: Teeth / Jenny Fretland VanVoorst and Maria Koran.
Description: New York, NY : AV2 by Weigl, [2017] | Series: All about your...
 | Includes bibliographical references and index.
Identifiers: LCCN 2016034657 (print) | LCCN 2016035349 (ebook) | ISBN
 9781489651587 (hard cover : alk. paper) | ISBN 9781489651594 (soft cover :
 alk. paper) | ISBN 9781489651600 (Multi-user ebk.)
Subjects: LCSH: Teeth--Juvenile literature.
Classification: LCC QM311 .F74 2017 (print) | LCC QM311 (ebook) | DDC
 612.3/11--dc23
LC record available at https://lccn.loc.gov/2016034657

Printed in the United States of America in Brainerd, Minnesota
1 2 3 4 5 6 7 8 9 0 20 19 18 17 16

082016
210716

Project Coordinator: Piper Whelan   Art Director: Terry Paulhus

Every reasonable effort has been made to trace ownership and to obtain permission to reprint copyright material. The publishers would be pleased to have any errors or omissions brought to their attention so that they may be corrected in subsequent printings.

Weigl acknowledges Getty Images, iStock, and Alamy as its primary image suppliers for this title.

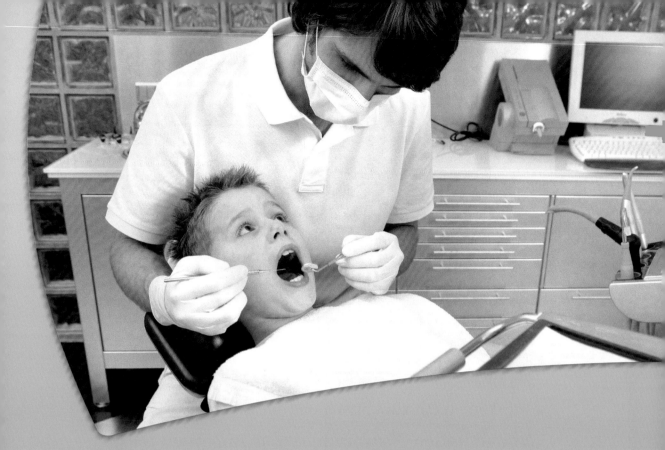

Contents

Chapter 1

What a Mouthful

Teeth help you eat. They also help you smile and speak. You probably do not think about your teeth a lot. Your teeth stay busy helping with digestion and communication. Your teeth have an important role in your daily life.

Chewing is the first step in the digestive process. This process begins when you take a bite of food. Your teeth cut and grind food into smaller pieces. These pieces travel to your stomach, where they are digested.

The words "dental" and "dentists" come from the root word *dent*. This means "tooth" in Latin.

Biting and chewing is important for breaking down food the body needs.

Teeth come in many different shapes. The tooth's shape helps it do its job. The four front teeth are called incisors. Incisors are on both the top and bottom jaws. These sharp teeth are made for cutting up food. On either side of the incisors are pointy teeth called canines. These teeth are like a dog's sharp fangs. In fact, the word "canine" comes from the Latin word for "dog." Canine teeth tear food into smaller pieces. There are two canine teeth on the top jaw and also on the bottom jaw.

After the canine teeth are the premolar teeth. These teeth are wider and have a flatter top. There are eight premolar teeth. Behind the premolar teeth are the molars. The molars are wider and flatter than the premolar teeth. Molars are used to grind food.

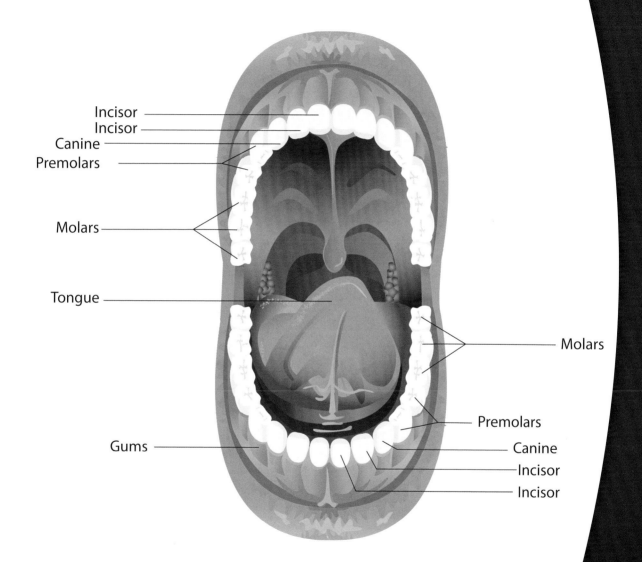

Incisor
Incisor
Canine
Premolars

Molars

Tongue

Molars

Premolars

Canine

Incisor

Incisor

Gums

Your teeth are great for chewing, but you also need them to talk. Your teeth work with your tongue and lips to form sounds. You could not say "tooth" correctly without your teeth. The tongue needs the front teeth to make the "th" sound. Without your teeth, the word would come out sounding like "toof."

Teeth help you talk so people can understand you. Teeth also help you communicate in other ways. The meaning behind a smile is always clear.

Keeping your teeth healthy also keeps your smile bright.

Some people have a hard time forming the right sounds for words. This is called a speech impediment.

Chapter 2

Getting to the Root

Most babies are born without teeth. Teeth start to come in when a baby is about six months old. By two years old, most kids have a full set of 20 teeth. These are called baby teeth.

Baby teeth are not permanent. As the body grows, so does the mouth. This makes room for more teeth in the mouth. Baby teeth are pushed out and replaced by permanent adult teeth. Most kids will have 28 permanent teeth by 12 years old. There are four other molars that could grow in. These molars are called wisdom teeth. Not everyone grows wisdom teeth. Adults with wisdom teeth have a full set of 32 teeth.

Most kids will lose their first tooth around the age of five.

Some adult animals, such as sharks, regrow teeth when they lose them. Humans have only one set of adult teeth. If you lose an adult tooth, it is gone for good.

Now we will get to the root of these 32 chompers. The outer part of a tooth is called the **crown**. It is the part everyone can see. You chew, smile, and talk using the crowns of your teeth. The crown is covered in a hard material called **enamel**. Enamel is the hardest material in your body. Enamel protects your inner tooth from the wear and tear of chewing. It also protects teeth from hot or cold. Without enamel, eating ice cream or drinking hot chocolate would be painful.

The crown covers a layer of bone-like material called **dentin**. Dentin surrounds and protects a soft inner **pulp**. The pulp contains a tooth's blood vessels and nerve endings. Blood vessels carry nutrients to a tooth. Nerves send messages to the brain to warn it about tooth problems. Pay attention to these messages. It is easier to fix a problem if you catch it early.

Your teeth are set into your jaw by roots. Front teeth have a single root. Molars have two or three roots. Gum tissue wraps around your jaw and the roots. It helps hold your teeth in place.

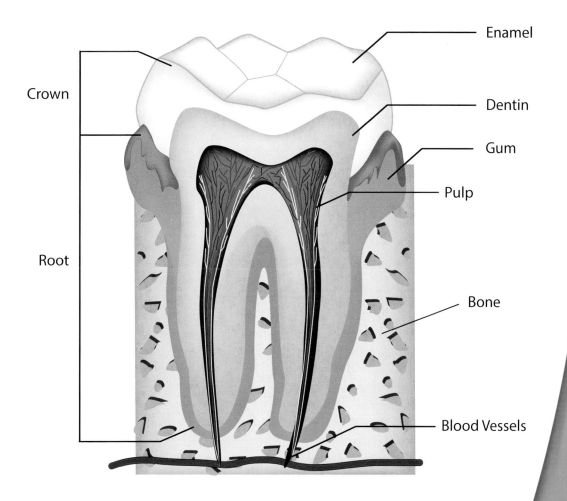

Crown

Root

Enamel

Dentin

Gum

Pulp

Bone

Blood Vessels

Chapter 3
When Good Teeth Go Bad

There is a lot going on in your mouth. **Bacteria** in your mouth are always looking for a good meal. Bacteria feed on scraps of food stuck between your teeth. As they feed, bacteria multiply. They group together to form a material called **plaque**. It sticks to your teeth and makes an acid. The acid eats through the enamel and causes the tooth to rot.

This rot creates a hole in the tooth. It is called a **cavity**. Cavities are a common tooth problem. They are usually easy to fix, too. The dentist removes the infected part using a drill. Then, the dentist fills the area with a material called **porcelain**. The porcelain blends in with the teeth. Some people get cavities more easily than others. Most people will have at least one cavity.

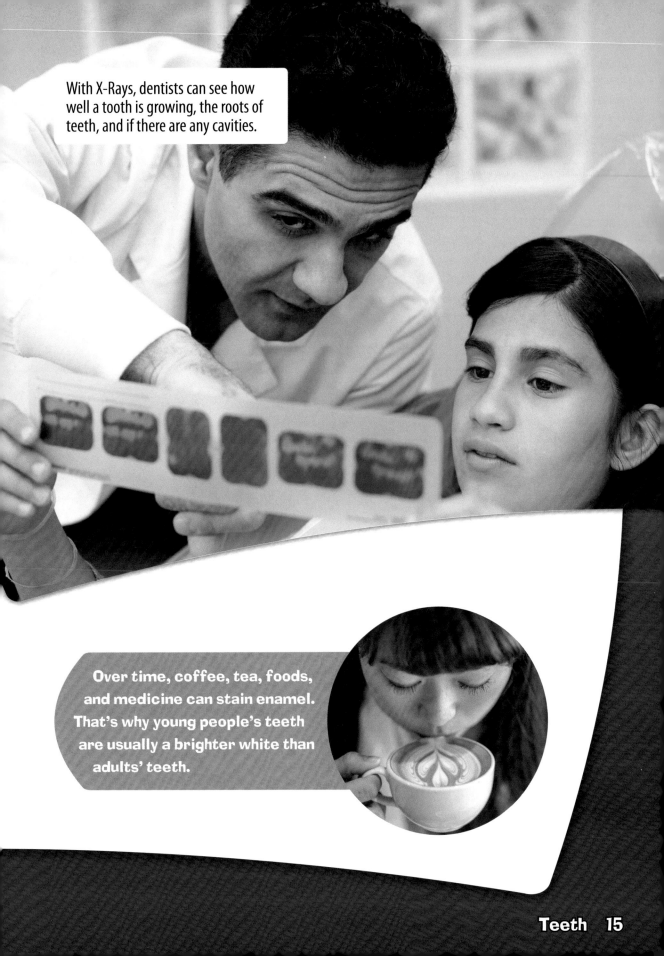

With X-Rays, dentists can see how well a tooth is growing, the roots of teeth, and if there are any cavities.

Over time, coffee, tea, foods, and medicine can stain enamel. That's why young people's teeth are usually a brighter white than adults' teeth.

Sometimes bacteria grow into the **gums** and attack gum tissue. This causes the gums to pull away from the teeth. It also creates a space where more bacteria can live. The problem becomes worse when this happens. Gum disease is more common in adults than children. Brushing the teeth more thoroughly and gently can treat gum disease.

Regular dentist visits, flossing, and brushing at an early age can prevent gum disease and cavities.

If orthodontia is needed, most kids start treatment between the ages of 9 and 14.

Teeth do not always fit the mouth they are in. They can be crowded or crooked. Teeth might not line up properly. This might make it hard to chew food, or make it awkward to smile much. Special dentists called **orthodontists** work on these problems. They may suggest wearing braces. These metal devices attach to the teeth and gently adjust them so they are straight and even. An orthodontist may also remove teeth. This will give crowded teeth extra space.

If an adult has wisdom teeth, they are often removed. Wisdom teeth cause problems when there is not enough space. It might be hard to fit four new teeth. Wisdom teeth also do not always come in straight.

Most tooth problems can be avoided with simple dental hygiene. Taking good care of your teeth will keep your smile healthy.

Before toothpaste was invented, people used ashes or chalk to clean their teeth.

Most dentists recommend brushing in a circular motion across and behind all teeth.

Chapter 4

Brush Up on Dental Care

Dental care is very important. The best tool for preventing tooth problems is your toothbrush. Choose a brush with soft bristles. They are the gentlest on your gums. Brush your teeth twice a day. Use toothpaste with fluoride, a mineral that strengthens tooth enamel. Make small circles over your teeth with your toothbrush. You should spend about three minutes brushing. Use dental floss to clean the areas between your teeth.

Food can have an effect on your dental health, too. Avoid candy and other sweets. Sweet foods cause more tooth decay than other foods. Brush right away after eating something sweet. Calcium helps keep teeth strong. Instead of sweets, eat foods like dairy products.

Calcium is important for healthy teeth, gums, and bones.

Visit a dentist twice a year. A dentist will check your teeth to catch any problems early. He or she will also clean your teeth. The dentist's special tools make your smile bright and sparkly.

Quiz

1. **What does the word "dent" mean in Latin?**

2. **What is the first step in the digestive process?**

3. **What are the four front teeth called?**

4. **What are the molars used for?**

5. **What animal can regrow its adult teeth?**

6. **How many baby teeth do most two-year-olds have?**

7. **What is the hard material covering the crown called?**

8. **What is a cavity?**

9. **What kind of dentist works to line up teeth properly, often using braces?**

10. **What did people use to clean their teeth before toothpaste was invented?**

Answers

1. TOOTH
2. CHEWING
3. THE INCISORS
4. THEY ARE USED TO GRIND FOOD
5. SHARKS
6. 20 TEETH
7. ENAMEL
8. A HOLE IN THE TOOTH CAUSED BY ACID EATING THROUGH THE ENAMEL
9. AN ORTHODONTIST
10. ASHES OR CHALK

Key Words

bacteria: microscopic living things that are all around you

cavity: a hole in something solid

crown: the top of something

dentin: the tooth material that surrounds and protects the pulp

enamel: the hard, white surface of your teeth

gums: the areas of pink flesh around the teeth

orthodontists: dentists who straighten uneven teeth

plaque: the coating made from food and bacteria

porcelain: the hard material used to fill dental cavities

pulp: the soft inner part of the tooth

Index

Log on to www.av2books.com

AV² by Weigl brings you media enhanced books that support active learning. Go to www.av2books.com, and enter the special code found on page 2 of this book. You will gain access to enriched and enhanced content that supplements and complements this book. Content includes video, audio, weblinks, quizzes, a slide show, and activities.

AV² Online Navigation

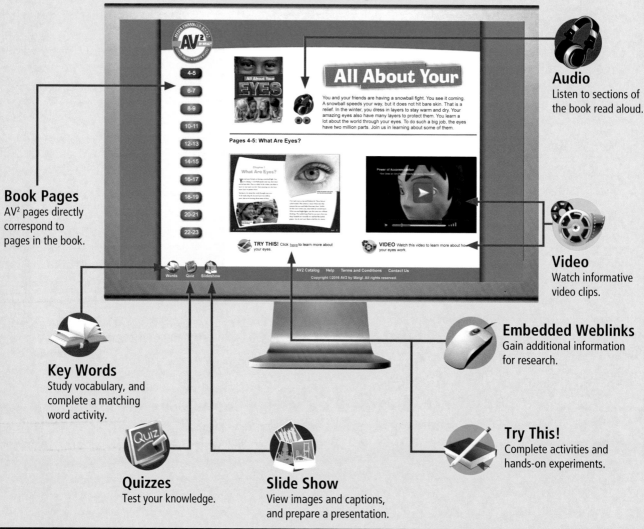

Audio
Listen to sections of the book read aloud.

Book Pages
AV² pages directly correspond to pages in the book.

Video
Watch informative video clips.

Key Words
Study vocabulary, and complete a matching word activity.

Embedded Weblinks
Gain additional information for research.

Quizzes
Test your knowledge.

Slide Show
View images and captions, and prepare a presentation.

Try This!
Complete activities and hands-on experiments.

AV² was built to bridge the gap between print and digital. We encourage you to tell us what you like and what you want to see in the future.

Sign up to be an AV² Ambassador at www.av2books.com/ambassador.